**Introducing SAM and his friends!**

# Spelling Made Easy at Home

**Helps you to read and spell**

Part of the best selling phonics series by
**Violet Brand**
with additional material by
**Katy Brand**

Violet Brand

Katy Brand

# Introduction

Violet Brand MBE wrote her highly successful 'Spelling Made Easy' series as a result of her work with young adults with reading difficulties between 1975 and 1980. She always maintained that *"The multi-sensory methods of teaching spelling seem to have been over-looked and too much emphasis has been placed on learning to spell through visual methods. The ears and the mouth have been forgotten and the power of the hand ignored."*

Her teaching and writing was always rooted in phonics, which has now become the accepted way to teach reading and spelling. Her classic 'Spelling Made Easy' books were published in 1984 but revised and updated in 2012 and now include the Synthetic Phonics sequence.

The stories in her books feature her own characters, Sam, Jim, Augustus (Gus) and Sue, Sam's wife. These have been illustrated for the first time with Violet's approval by leading TV Animator Richard Ollive.

Consequently BrandBooks are now able to publish this illustrated 'Spelling Made Easy at Home' series which mirrors exactly the word lists and stories in the Revised Spelling Made Easy Teacher books At the end of each book there is an additional story by Katy Brand, Violet's granddaughter and a highly successful TV comedy actor and writer, featuring all the sounds used in the book.

**These books are therefore ideal for children to use at home.**

BrandBooks 2013
*www.spellingmadeeasy.co.uk*

© All rights assigned to BrandBooks (a division of Spelling Made Easy Ltd.) and Violet Brand and Katy Brand who assert their moral rights as the authors.

ISBN 978-1-904421-245 All rights reserved. www.spellingmadeeasy.co.uk

The copyright of all materials in the 'Spelling Made Easy' series remains the property of the publisher and the authors.

No part of this book or illustrations may be reproduced or translated in any form or by any means, electronic or mechanical, including recording or by an information storage or retrieval system without permission in writing from the publisher.

### Contents

| Pages | |
|---|---|
| 4 — 23 | Sam's sounds and stories |
| 24 — 31 | Sam and the Horse |

### Things to do

- Use the spaces next to Sam's words to copy them.
- Draw your own pictures in the empty boxes as marked.
- Write in your answers to the questions about the story in the second part of the book.

*Spelling Made Easy at Home Red Book 1 is part of the Spelling Made Easy Series by Violet Brand with additional material by Katy Brand. Original characters drawn by Richard Ollive.*

First published in the United Kingdom in 2013.

# Sam's 'a' words

This is Sam saying 'a'
Look at the shape of his mouth.
Now you make the sound and feel the shape of your mouth.

| at _____ | cat _____ | hat _____ |
| fat _____ | ran _____ | dam _____ |
| sat _____ | gas _____ | sad _____ |
| Sam _____ | Gran _____ | bad _____ |
| mat _____ | bag _____ | van _____ |
| tap _____ | nap _____ | lap _____ |
| pan _____ | man _____ | flat _____ |

HELP!
Sam's new words:
the, is, he, on

# Sam's 'a' story

The fat man is Sam.

Sam sat on the hat. He is sad.

Can you draw a picture of Sam?

# Sam's 'o' words

This is Sam saying 'o'
Look at the shape of his mouth.
Now you make the sound and feel the shape of your mouth.

| o n  _____ | h o p  _____ |
| d o g  _____ | s t o p  _____ |
| c o t  _____ | b o x  _____ |
| h o t  _____ | f o x  _____ |
| t o p  _____ | s o ft  _____ |

HELP!
Sam's new word:
of

# Sam's 'o' story

Sam had a b**o**x of h**o**t-d**o**gs.

The d**o**g sat **o**n t**o**p.

*Can you draw a picture of a h**o**t-d**o**g?*

# Sam's 'i' words

This is Sam saying 'i'
Look at the shape of his mouth.
Now you make the sound and feel the shape of your mouth.

| | |
|---|---|
| in _____ | his _____ |
| big _____ | pig _____ |
| bit _____ | six _____ |
| hit _____ | win _____ |
| sit _____ | wind _____ |
| lip _____ | milk _____ |
| him _____ | hit _____ |
| Jim _____ | zip _____ |
| | drink _____ |

# Sam's 'i' story

The dog bit the pig.
Sam hits him.

The dog sits.

Can you draw a picture of the dog and the pig?

# Sam's 'e' words

This is Sam saying 'e'
Look at the shape of his mouth.
Now you make the sound and feel the shape of your mouth.

b e d  _____  y e t  _____
h e n  _____  h e l p  _____
l e g  _____  n e s t  _____
r e d  _____  w e n t  _____
t e n  _____  s l e p t  _____

# Sam's 'e' story

The red hen slept in a wet nest.

The dog slept in a box and Sam slept in a big, soft bed.

Can you draw a picture of the red hen in a wet nest?

# Sam's 'u' words

This is Sam saying 'u'
Look at the shape of his mouth.
Now you make the sound and feel the shape of your mouth.

| b u s  _____ | j u m p  _____ |
| c u p  _____ | r u n  _____ |
| f u n  _____ | u p  _____ |
| s u n  _____ | m u s t  _____ |
| m u d  _____ | m u m p s  _____ |

# Sam's 'u' story

Sam r**u**ns to stop the b**u**s.
His dog j**u**mps **u**p.

Sam sits in the m**u**d.

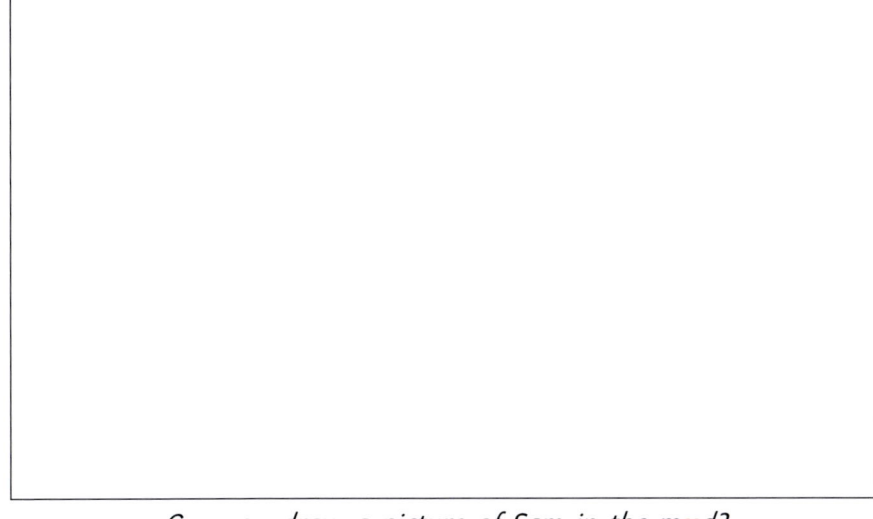

Can you draw a picture of Sam in the m**u**d?

# Sam's 'ck' words

This is Sam saying 'ck'
Look at the shape of his mouth.
Now you make the sound and feel the shape of your mouth.

| back  _____ | sick   _____ |
|---|---|
| lick  _____ | sock   _____ |
| kick  _____ | stick  _____ |
| pick  _____ | stuck  _____ |
| neck  _____ | smack  _____ |

# Sam's 'ck' story

Stop the bus.

Sam is stuck in the mud.
Six men must pick him up.

*Can you draw a picture of six men and Sam?*

# Sam's 'ee' words

This is Sam saying '**ee**'
Look at the shape of his mouth.
Now you make the sound and feel the shape of your mouth.

f**ee**t _____    gr**ee**n _____
s**ee** _____    k**ee**p _____
m**ee**t _____    sl**ee**p _____
tr**ee** _____    sw**ee**t _____
fr**ee** _____    thr**ee** _____
qu**ee**n _____

# Sam's 'ee' story

Sam sucks lots of fr**ee** gr**ee**n sw**ee**ts.
He f**ee**ls sick.

His dog just sl**ee**ps.

*Can you draw a picture of a dog asl**ee**p?*

# Sam's 'oo' words

This is Sam saying 'oo'     This is Sam saying 'oo' (u)
Look at the shape of his mouth.
Now you make the sound and feel the shape of your mouth.

### oo
food _____
moon _____
room _____
soon _____
spoon _____
zoo _____

### oo (u)
cook _____
look _____
foot _____
good _____

# Sam's 'oo' story

Sam cooks lots of good, hot food.

The dog soon looks in the room.

Can you draw a picture of good, hot food?

# Sam's 'ar' words

This is Sam saying '**ar**'
Look at the shape of his mouth.
Now you make the sound and feel the shape of your mouth.

c**ar** _____        st**ar** _____
f**ar** _____        b**ar**k _____
p**ar**k _____       t**ar**t _____
d**ar**k _____       sc**ar**f _____
j**ar** _____

# Sam's 'ar' story

It is d**ar**k in the c**ar**.
Sam sits on the jam t**ar**t.

His dog jumps up and b**ar**ks.

Can you draw a picture of Sam on the jam t**ar**t?

# Sam's 'or' words

This is Sam saying '**or**'
Look at the shape of his mouth.
Now you make the sound and feel the shape of your mouth.

f**o**rk _____     f**o**r _____
c**o**rk _____     h**o**rse _____
p**o**rt _____     st**o**rm _____
c**o**rn _____     sp**o**rt _____

# Sam's 'or' story

The st**or**m is bad.
The dog and the h**or**se run.

Sam runs, but it is hard for him.
He gets wet.

Can you draw a picture of Sam in a bad st**or**m?

# Sam and the horse

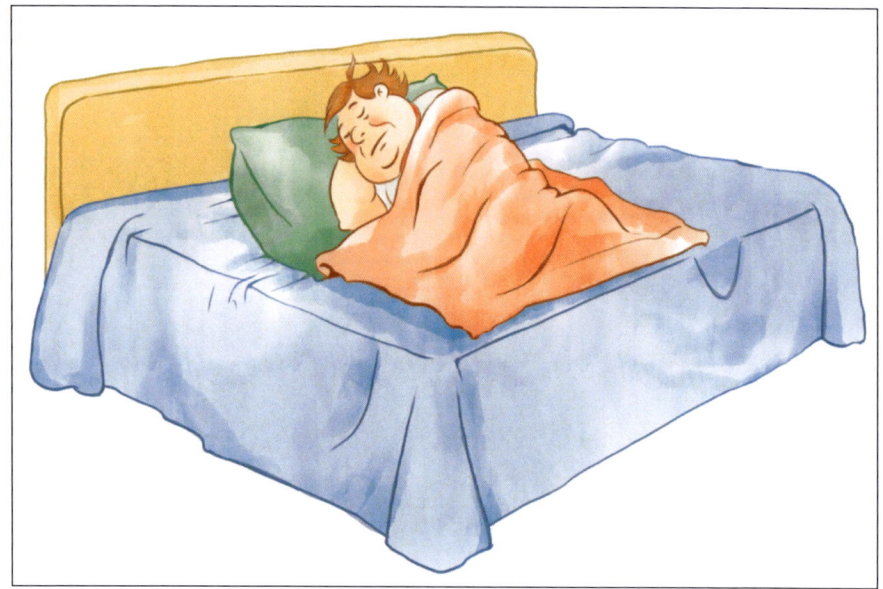

This is Sam in bed.

Sam is a man. Sam is in his bed. His cat is on top of the bed. His big dog is in a box. The big dog sat up and bit the cat on the leg. The cat did yelp and Sam sat up in his bed. The cat ran from the bed, and from the man and the dog. The dog ran from the bed. Sam must run to stop the dog and the cat. The sun is not up but Sam, the dog and the cat must run. Sam's pig is in the mud. The cat runs to the pig. Sam runs into the mud. It is not fun!

*Use the story to fill in the gaps.*

Sam is a _____.
Sam slept in his _____.
The cat slept on _____ of the bed.
The dog _____ in a box.
The dog is _____.
The dog _____ the cat.
Sam must _____ to stop the cat.
The _____ is not up.
The cat runs to the _____.


*Can you draw a picture of Sam in his bed?*

# Sam and the horse

This is Sam with a stick and a cup of milk.

Sam must get a big bag to stop the cat. The cat runs to the red hen. A fox stops the cat. The red hen sits on the nest and six eggs. The fox wets its lips. Sam must stop the fox and the cat. He gets a stick and a cup of milk. Sam claps his hands and the fox and the cat stop. The fox runs but the cat gets the cup of milk. The dog gets the stick. The sun is up but Sam has not slept. He is hot. He runs up to his soft bed. He will miss the bus!

*Use the story to fill in the gaps.*

Sam gets a _____ bag.
Sam must _____ the cat.
The cat _____ to the hen.
The _____ is red.
A fox stops the _____.
The hen _____ on the nest.
The fox _____ its lips.
Sam gets a _____ of milk.
The dog gets the _____.
Sam runs to his _____ bed.


Can you draw a picture of Sam with a stick and a cup of milk?

# Sam and the horse

Sam with a bag of crisps, a fork and the corn.

The bus has left and Sam is still in his bed! He is asleep. The dog barks and the cat yelps. Sam sits up in his bed. He looks at the clock and jumps up. He must meet a man! The bus has left and Sam has no car. He must meet the man in the park. He can jog, but Sam is not good at sport. He is a bit fat and has a bad back. Sam needs food. He looks in his room. He can see some sweets in a jar, a jam tart in a box, a bag of crisps and corn. The sweets are no good and he must cook the corn with a spoon. Sam grabs the bag of crisps. He picks up a fork and the corn. He runs to meet the man at the big tree in the park.

*Use the story to fill in the gaps.*

The dog _____.
Sam _____ at the clock.
Sam must _____ a man.
Sam has no _____.
Sam is not good at _____.
Sam has a bad _____.
Sam keeps _____ in a jar.
Sam has a bag of _____.
Sam must _____ the corn.
Sam _____ up a fork.

Can you draw a picture of Sam's sweets in a jar?

# Sam and the horse

Sam on the back of the horse.

The park is very far and Sam must meet the man at three o'clock. It will be three o'clock soon and Sam must run. Sam feels sick but he must run to meet the man. Sam sees a horse from the farm. He jumps on top of its back. The horse looks up at Sam. Sam kicks and the horse runs. Sam must keep his hands on the horse's neck. He must keep his legs and feet free to stop the horse. Soon, Sam can see the park. He can see the man he must meet. The man can see Sam. Sam stops the horse and jumps from its back. Sam pats the horse. It has been good. The horse needs food. Sam feeds the horse the corn.

*Use the story to fill in the gaps.*

The _____ is very far.
Sam must meet the man at _____ o'clock.
It will be three o'clock _____.
Sam feels _____.
Sam sees a _____.
The horse is from the _____.
Sam must keep his _____ free to stop the horse.
Sam puts his hands on the horse's _____.
The horse has been _____.
Sam feeds it the _____.

Can you draw a picture of Sam as he feeds the horse with corn?

### Red Home Books — Introductory Level

Book 1 ISBN 978-1-904421-245
Book 2 ISBN 978-1-904421-252
Book 3 ISBN 978-1-904421-269
Book 4 ISBN 978-1-904421-276

### Green Home Books — Level 1

Book 1 ISBN 978-1-904421-283
Book 2 ISBN 978-1-904421-290
Book 3 ISBN 978-1-904421-306
Book 4 ISBN 978-1-904421-313

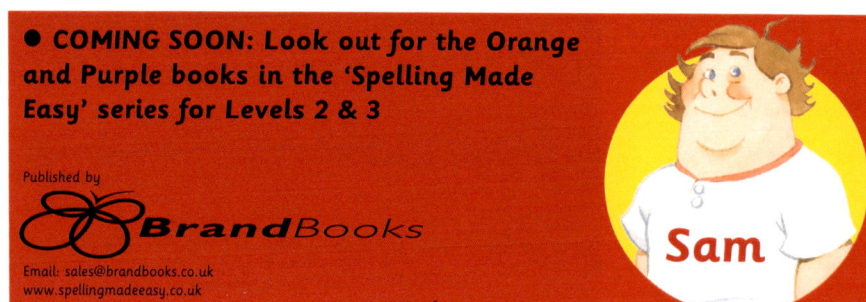

● COMING SOON: Look out for the Orange and Purple books in the 'Spelling Made Easy' series for Levels 2 & 3

Published by
**Brand**Books

Email: sales@brandbooks.co.uk
www.spellingmadeeasy.co.uk